THE NEW ORLEANS SAINTS

BY JOANNE MATTERN

EPIC

BELLWETHER MEDIA ★ MINNEAPOLIS, MN

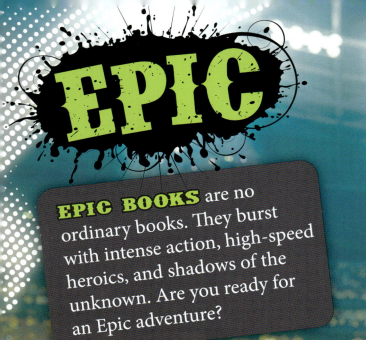

EPIC BOOKS are no ordinary books. They burst with intense action, high-speed heroics, and shadows of the unknown. Are you ready for an Epic adventure?

This book is intended for educational use. Organization and franchise logos are trademarks of the National Football League (NFL). This is not an official book of the NFL. It is not approved by or connected with the NFL.

This edition first published in 2024 by Bellwether Media, Inc.

No part of this publication may be reproduced in whole or in part without written permission of the publisher. For information regarding permission, write to Bellwether Media, Inc., Attention: Permissions Department, 6012 Blue Circle Drive, Minnetonka, MN 55343.

Library of Congress Cataloging-in-Publication Data

Names: Mattern, Joanne, 1963- author.
Title: The New Orleans Saints / by Joanne Mattern.
Description: Minneapolis, MN : Bellwether Media, 2024. | Series: Epic. NFL team profiles | Includes bibliographical references and index. | Audience: Ages 7-12 | Audience: Grades 2-3 | Summary: "Engaging images accompany information about the New Orleans Saints. The combination of high-interest subject matter and light text is intended for students in grades 2 through 7" -- Provided by publisher.
Identifiers: LCCN 2023021992 (print) | LCCN 2023021993 (ebook) | ISBN 9798886874884 (library binding) | ISBN 9798886876765 (ebook)
Subjects: LCSH: New Orleans Saints (Football team)--History--Juvenile literature.
Classification: LCC GV956.N366 M37 2024 (print) | LCC GV956.N366 (ebook) | DDC 796.332/640976335--dc23/eng/20230511
LC record available at https://lccn.loc.gov/2023021992
LC ebook record available at https://lccn.loc.gov/2023021993

Text copyright © 2024 by Bellwether Media, Inc. EPIC and associated logos are trademarks and/or registered trademarks of Bellwether Media, Inc.

Editor: Betsy Rathburn   Designer: Jeffrey Kollock

Printed in the United States of America, North Mankato, MN.

TABLE OF CONTENTS

GRAB AND RUN!	4
THE HISTORY OF THE SAINTS	6
THE SAINTS TODAY	14
GAME DAY!	16
NEW ORLEANS SAINTS FACTS	20
GLOSSARY	22
TO LEARN MORE	23
INDEX	24

GRAB AND RUN!

TRACY PORTER

The Saints face the Colts in **Super Bowl** 44. Saints **cornerback** Tracy Porter **intercepts** a pass. He runs 74 yards for a **touchdown**.

The Saints go on to win the Super Bowl!

5

THE HISTORY OF THE SAINTS

In 1966, the National Football League (NFL) started a new team in New Orleans, Louisiana. The Saints were announced on November 1. This is a holiday called All Saints' Day.

Fans were very excited. The team played its first game in 1967.

1967 SAINTS GAME

A SPECIAL SONG

The Saints are named after a song called "When the Saints Go Marching In." The song is by Louis Armstrong. He was born in New Orleans.

1967 SAINTS GAME

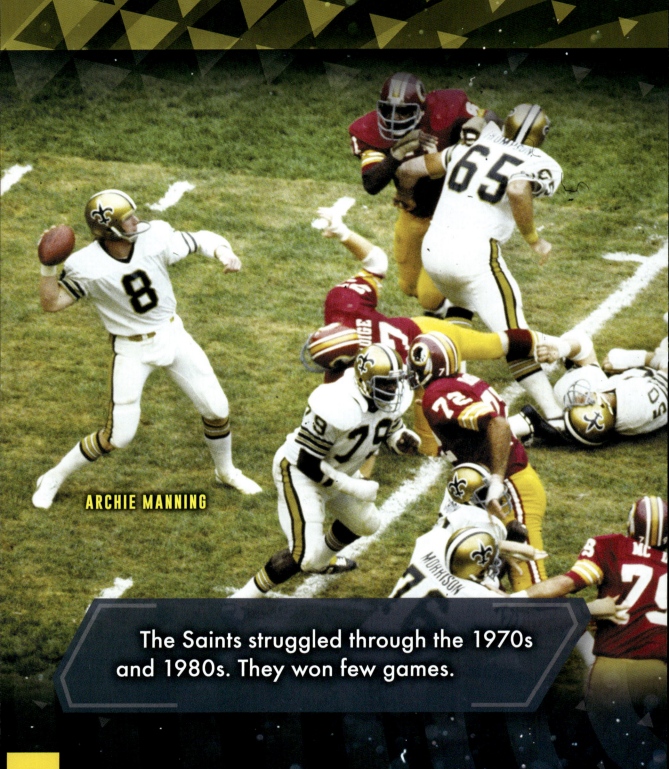

ARCHIE MANNING

The Saints struggled through the 1970s and 1980s. They won few games.

RICKEY JACKSON

The team did not have a winning season until 1987. But they had great players like **quarterback** Archie Manning and **linebacker** Rickey Jackson.

The team had little success in the 1990s and 2000s. They rarely made the **playoffs**.

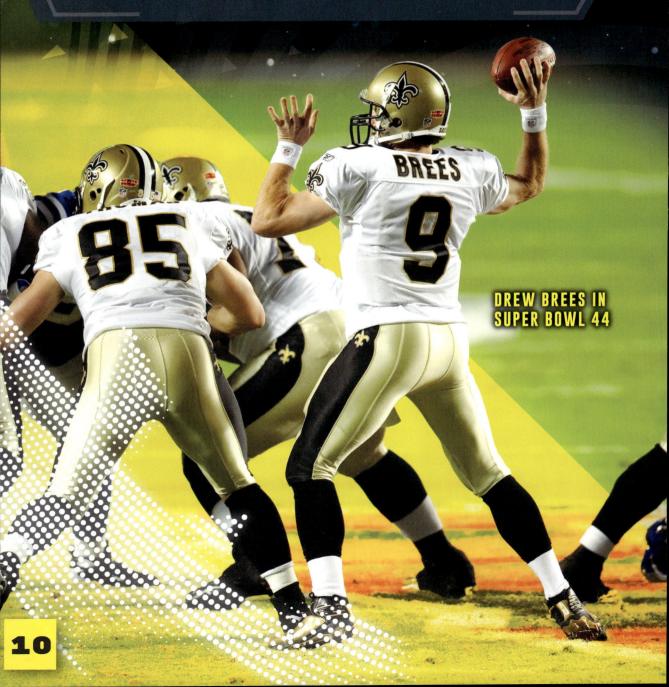

DREW BREES IN SUPER BOWL 44

In 2010, the Saints won their first Super Bowl. Quarterback Drew Brees led the team. They beat the Indianapolis Colts 31–17!

TROPHY CASE

NFC WEST championships
2

NFC championships
1

SUPER BOWL championships
1

NFC SOUTH championships
7

The Saints did well in the 2010s. They made the playoffs in six seasons.

2016 SAINTS

In 2017, **running back** Alvin Kamara joined the team. He helped them reach the playoffs four years in a row. The Saints hope for even more success in the future!

ALVIN KAMARA

THE SAINTS TODAY

SAINTS VS. FALCONS

The Saints play in the NFC South. Their **stadium** is the Caesars Superdome. It is in New Orleans, Louisiana.

The Saints' biggest **rival** is the Atlanta Falcons. Sparks fly when these two teams meet!

📍 LOCATION 📍

CAESARS SUPERDOME
New Orleans, Louisiana

LOUISIANA

GAME DAY!

Fans fill the Superdome on game day. They dress in black and gold.

A player leads fans in a special cheer. Everyone yells "Who Dat?" to get ready for the game.

RING THE BELL

Since 2022, home games start in a fun way. Former Saints players ring a special bell three times before kickoff!

CAESARS SUPERDOME

17

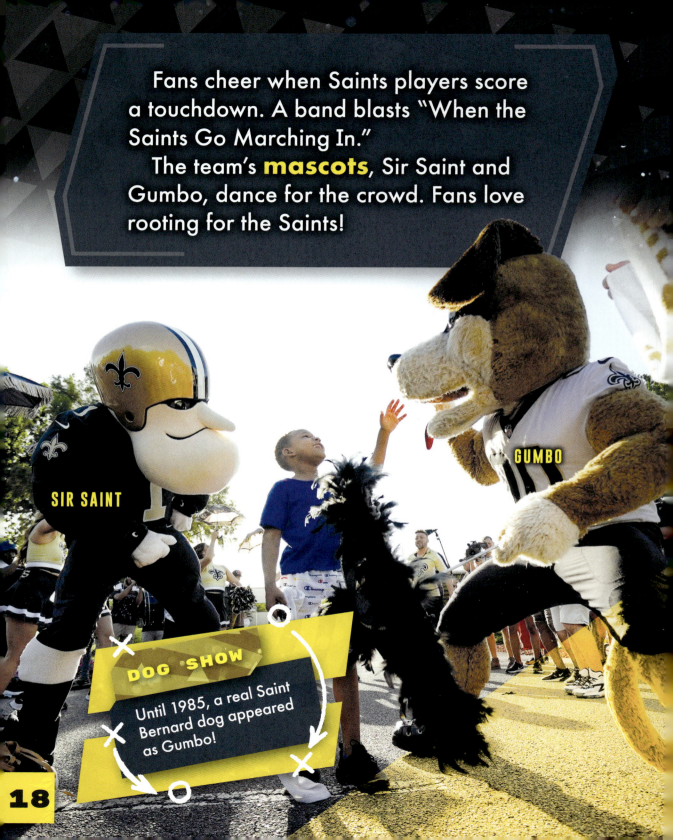

Fans cheer when Saints players score a touchdown. A band blasts "When the Saints Go Marching In."

The team's **mascots**, Sir Saint and Gumbo, dance for the crowd. Fans love rooting for the Saints!

SIR SAINT

GUMBO

DOG SHOW

Until 1985, a real Saint Bernard dog appeared as Gumbo!

18

★ FAMOUS PLAYERS

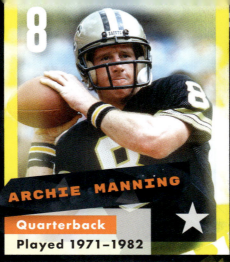

8

ARCHIE MANNING
Quarterback
Played 1971–1982

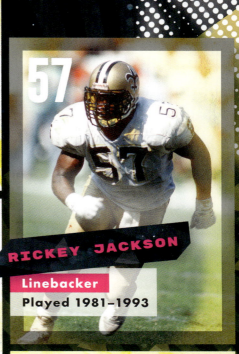

57

RICKEY JACKSON
Linebacker
Played 1981–1993

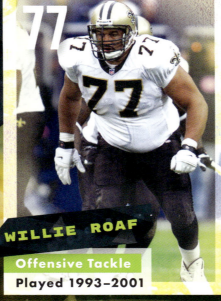

77

WILLIE ROAF
Offensive Tackle
Played 1993–2001

12

MARQUES COLSTON
Wide Receiver
Played 2006–2015

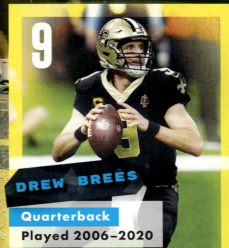

9

DREW BREES
Quarterback
Played 2006–2020

NEW ORLEANS SAINTS FACTS

LOGO

JOINED THE NFL	1967

NICKNAME	The Who Dats

MASCOTS

SIR SAINT AND GUMBO

CONFERENCE
National Football Conference (NFC)

COLORS

DIVISION | NFC South

Atlanta Falcons

Carolina Panthers

Tampa Bay Buccaneers

STADIUM

★ **CAESARS SUPERDOME** ★

opened August 3, 1975

holds **74,295** people

20

⏱ TIMELINE

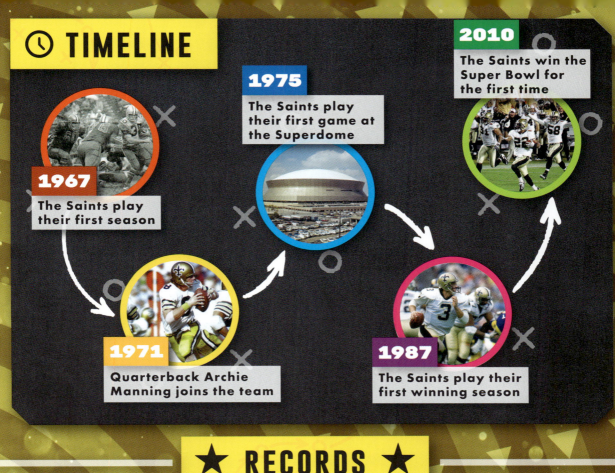

1967 — The Saints play their first season

1971 — Quarterback Archie Manning joins the team

1975 — The Saints play their first game at the Superdome

1987 — The Saints play their first winning season

2010 — The Saints win the Super Bowl for the first time

★ RECORDS ★

All-Time Passing Leader
Drew Brees
68,010 yards

All-Time Rushing Leader
Mark Ingram
6,500 yards

All-Time Receiving Leader
Marques Colston
9,759 yards

All-Time Scoring Leader
Morten Andersen
1,318 points

21

GLOSSARY

cornerback—a player whose main job is to stop players on the other team from catching the ball

intercepts—catches a pass thrown by the opposing team

linebacker—a player whose main job is to tackle opposing players

mascots—animals or symbols that represent a sports team

playoffs—games played after the regular season is over; playoff games determine which teams play in the championship game.

quarterback—a player whose main job is to throw and hand off the ball

rival—a long-standing opponent

running back—a player whose main job is to run with the ball

stadium—an arena where sports are played

Super Bowl—the annual championship game of the NFL

touchdown—a score that occurs when a team crosses into their opponent's end zone with the football; a touchdown is worth six points.

TO LEARN MORE

AT THE LIBRARY

Coleman, Ted. *New Orleans Saints*. Mendota Heights, Minn.: Press Room Editions, 2021.

Meier, William. *New Orleans Saints*. Minneapolis, Minn.: Abdo Publishing, 2020.

Rea, Amy C. *Falcons vs. Saints*. Minnetonka, Minn.: Kaleidoscope Pub., 2019.

ON THE WEB

FACTSURFER

Factsurfer.com gives you a safe, fun way to find more information.

1. Go to www.factsurfer.com.

2. Enter "New Orleans Saints" into the search box and click 🔍.

3. Select your book cover to see a list of related content.

INDEX

All Saints' Day, 6
Armstrong, Louis, 7
bell, 17
Brees, Drew, 10, 11
Caesars Superdome, 14, 15, 16, 17, 20
cheer, 16, 18
colors, 16, 20
famous players, 19
fans, 6, 16, 18
history, 4, 5, 6, 8, 9, 10, 11, 12, 13, 17, 18
Jackson, Rickey, 9
Kamara, Alvin, 13
Manning, Archie, 8, 9
mascots, 18, 20
name, 7

National Football League (NFL), 6, 20
New Orleans, Louisiana, 6, 7, 14, 15
New Orleans Saints facts, 20–21
NFC South, 14, 20
playoffs, 10, 12, 13
Porter, Tracy, 4
positions, 4, 9, 11, 13
records, 21
rival, 15
Super Bowl, 4, 5, 10, 11
timeline, 21
trophy case, 11
"When the Saints Go Marching In," 7, 18

The images in this book are reproduced through the courtesy of: Sean Gardner/ Getty Images, front cover; Sean Xu, front cover (stadium); All-Pro Reels/ Wikipedia, p. 3; Paul Spinelli/ AP Images, p. 4; PCN Photography/ Alamy, p. 5; Jack Thornell/ AP Images, p. 6; Diamond Images/ Getty Images, pp. 6-7; Nate Fine/ Getty Images, p. 8; George Rose/ Getty Images, p. 9; Paul Abell/ AP Images, pp. 10-11; Wesley Hitt/ Getty Images, p. 12; Dustin Satloff/ Getty Images, pp. 12-13; Peter G. Forest/ AP Images, p. 14; Kirby Lee/ AP Images, p. 15; NFL/ Wikipedia, pp. 15 (logo), 20 (logos); Rick Scuteri/ AP Images, p. 16; Sean Gardner/ AP Images, pp. 16-17; Gerald Herbert/ AP Images, pp. 18-19, 20 (mascot); Focus On Sport/ Getty Images, pp. 19 (Archie Manning, Rickey Jackson), 21 (Morten Andersen); Icon Sportswire/ Getty Images, p. 19 (Willie Roaf); Stacy Revere/ Getty Images, p. 19 (Marques Colston); Cooper Neill, p. 19 (Drew Brees); William A. Morgan, p. 20 (stadium); Bettmann/ Getty Images, p. 21 (1967); James Flores/ Getty Images, p. 21 (1971); ClassicStock/ Getty Images, p. 21 (1975); Owen C. Shaw/ Getty Images, p. 21 (1987); Jed Jacobsohn/ Getty Images, p. 21 (2010); Chris Graythen/ Getty Images, p. 21 (Drew Brees); Tribune Content Agency LLC/ Alamy, p. 21 (Mark Ingram); REUTERS/ Alamy, p. 21 (Marques Colton); Dustin Satloff/ Getty Images, p. 23.